MARTIN McGUINNESS

HENRY McDONALD

MARTIN McGUINNESS

A LIFE REMEMBERED

·THE·
BLACK
·STAFF·
PRESS

First published in 2017 by
Blackstaff Press
an imprint of Colourpoint Creative Limited
Colourpoint House
21 Jubilee Road
Newtownards
Northern Ireland
BT23 4YH

Printed in Italy by Rotolito Lombarda S.p.A.

A CIP catalogue record for this book is
available from the British Library

ISBN 978 1 78073 168 1

www.blackstaffpress.com

Contents

Introduction

In politics, as in life, the word 'journey' is overused and hackneyed. But when it comes to Martin McGuinness's story, there is no word more apposite to describe his remarkable trajectory from butcher's apprentice and IRA militant to deputy first minister.

Observers from all over the world considering the development of the Northern Ireland peace process have seen McGuinness as the embodiment of how an entire society can not only survive, but ultimately find a way to move beyond, decades of violent political conflict. Indeed McGuinness was sought after by governments and insurgents, by both state and non-state actors, in other conflict zones around the globe. He travelled with former Ulster Volunteer Force bomber-turned-politician David Ervine to Sri Lanka, for example, to try to encourage the development of a peace process between the Sinhalese government and the Tamil Tigers.

This photographic collection is, in a sense, a series of milestones on the often bloody road from armed conflict to a peaceful resolution, of sorts, that is unique in the world.

The book begins in 1968 in Derry, where Martin McGuinness was born in 1950 and where he grew up. The opening photographs show the re-eruption of the Troubles as state forces respond brutally to the civil rights marches. Images of the police beating peaceful protesters with batons were beamed all over the world, and brought widespread condemnation of Northern Ireland's unionist government.

Photographs of state violence and street-level resistance give way to images of the Parachute Regiment in Derry in 1972, and of Bloody Sunday, in which thirteen unarmed civilians died on 30 January of that year. Within months of that atrocity, reports emerge of an emboldened Provisional IRA in the city, bulging with a fresh wave of recruits, hell-bent on revenge.

What is most striking about the first images to appear of Martin McGuinness himself – who in the stormy atmosphere of the early Troubles had risen rapidly up the ranks of the IRA – is their open, bold nature. There is the infamous picture of McGuinness posing with a version of the old German Luger pistol in May 1972. A month later McGuinness is pictured at a PIRA press conference alongside the founding fathers of the Provisionals – Dáithí Ó Conaill, Seán Mac Stíofáin and Seamus Twomey, the latter being one of the strategists of the organisation's car bombing campaign which caused so much carnage a few weeks later on Bloody Friday, when nine civilians died and over one hundred were injured when multiple bombs exploded across Belfast.

As we move from black and white to colour McGuinness's life follows a path that takes in a conviction for IRA membership in Dublin's Special Criminal Court in 1973; an unsuccessful attempt to prosecute him on the same charge north of the border in 1976; the 1981 hunger strike; and onwards towards his deepening involvement in Sinn Féin's political rise from the early 1980s. From here on, we see McGuinness as politician – albeit one who in his fledgling years was an advocate–apologist for the IRA's violence. It is this record that makes him, even in death, such a divisive figure for so many, both in Northern Ireland and further afield.

To the families of informers like Frank Hegarty, McGuinness was the Judas goat who – according to Hegarty's mother, Rose – persuaded her to urge her son to return from protective exile in England to Derry. Having been talked into coming home, Hegarty was found outside Castlederg in County Tyrone with bullet wounds in the back of his head. Until the day of her death, Rose Hegarty claimed McGuinness had sworn to her that her son would be safe if he came back to Derry.

The widow of Patsy Gillespie has expressed regret that she never had the opportunity to question McGuinness about her husband's death and to ask why he had been considered a 'legitimate target'. Patsy Gillespie, a Catholic civilian who worked at a Derry army camp, was used as a 'human bomb' – he was strapped into a van loaded with explosives and forced to drive to the army checkpoint at Coshquin, an incident in which he and five soldiers died. For her, as for so many of the loved ones of the 1,800 victims of the IRA, McGuinness will remain one of the 'unforgiven'. He never apologised for the three and a half decades of carnage, which ended up not with a united Ireland in his lifetime but an internal political settlement akin to the one McGuinness and his comrades were happy to see destroyed (thanks to loyalist and unionist opposition in the main) back in 1974.

For the rank and file of the mainstream republican movement, though, he remains forever a hero and a 'solider' of their struggle, as indicated on his gravestone by the word óglach. For the majority of the nationalist electorate in Northern Ireland there would have been no peace process without McGuinness at the helm, and he is widely lauded and deeply admired for delivering that. From some of his old foes and former critics there is respect – some of it grudging, much of it admiring – for the way he managed, alongside Adams, to turn around an organisation so deftly from its armed campaign towards peaceful politics and historic compromise. For global onlookers – particularly would-be statesmen trapped in other seemingly intractable conflicts – McGuinness was among those who provided a template for peacemaking across the world.

These foreign observers saw a man of war transformed into a man of peace, who in his later years forged once-unthinkable friendships, first with Ian Paisley and later with Peter Robinson. They marvelled at this one-time senior IRA commander meeting Queen Elizabeth II.

One veteran of the IRA's Derry Brigade, whose record in the organisation includes arms buying abroad for the movement and periods of imprisonment, has suggested McGuinness was doubting the efficacy of the IRA's armed campaign as far back as the late 1980s. He recalls an alleged incident in 1987 when he was driving McGuinness to County Monaghan to the funeral of one of the eight-man-strong IRA unit killed by the British Army's Special Air Service outside Loughgall RUC station that year.

'I had driven Martin down from Derry and we were heading towards the British army checkpoint at Aughnacloy. As we waited in a line of traffic for the inevitable checks and hassles from the Brits, Martin said something very strange to me. He said, "Do you ever wonder what this all about? Did you ever think, what's achieved by shooting some off-duty UDR man or cop while they're out delivering milk or working on their farm?" At the time I was worried that when he said this he was just testing me; that he was trying to see if I was still loyal to the armed struggle. I kept my mouth shut and said nothing. But after all that has happened in the last two decades I wonder now if he was trying to tell me something significant,' the ex-IRA prisoner and activist said. (It should be stated that the IRA veteran who conveyed this story has become disillusioned with Sinn Féin's political direction and has sided with the republican dissident cause.)

This anecdote has to be set against the fact that at this time McGuinness was still describing the IRA's armed campaign in unapologetic terms as 'the cutting edge' of republican struggle. It had been only two years earlier, in 1985, when McGuinness appeared in the controversial BBC series *Real Lives: At the Edge of the Union*, claiming that winning elections alone would not in his mind bring 'freedom in Ireland'.

Throughout the often stumbling, at times rancorous, inter-party negotiations and discussions McGuinness was central to – from the 1994 IRA ceasefire to the Good Friday Agreement four years later – the personal qualities that helped him command such respect within his own movement came across, even to his old enemies in unionism. His personality and ability to work a room, even to disarm his opponents with charm, should not be underestimated. He could also be self-deprecating, even on very public occasions.

When the first power-sharing executive since 1974 sat down to do business in November 1999 the participants – unionists, nationalists and republicans – posed for a 'class photograph' around the cabinet table. McGuinness mistakenly took the seat allocated to the Ulster Unionist minister Michael McGimpsey. When David Trimble spotted that Sinn Féin's chief negotiator was in the wrong place he called out, 'Hello, Mr McGimpsey, hello McGimpsey.' Noticing his error, McGuinness smiled over to Trimble and replied, 'Trust me to be the first one to make a mistake.' His response provoked further smiles around the table, even amongst his one-time enemies.

Two years later, on a speaking tour of North America, he was once mistaken by an audience member for a famous American broadcaster. 'Are you David Letterman?' the woman asked, to which McGuinness replied, 'Well, at home they think I'm Art Garfunkel.'

One senior Northern Ireland civil servant who worked with McGuinness when he was minister of education in the first post-Good Friday Agreement devolved government also attested to his ability to quickly absorb complex position papers and policy documents. 'You could brief him on some policy position or problem concerning education and he could note it down on a single sheet, and instantly show that he had grasped it,' the now-retired civil servant remembered.

One year after the Good Friday Agreement was signed the fragile power-sharing government at Stormont was in deep trouble. Once again, Senator George Mitchell was called in to help, and he took the parties out of Northern Ireland and over to the US ambassador's residence in London. Within a few hours it became evident that out of the hothouse of Belfast a rapport was developing between the key players.

There was a telling moment regarding McGuinness as the party leaders sat down for an evening meal in the American ambassador's house. Just before the starters were brought out, the former IRA Old Bailey bomber Gerry Kelly leaned over the table and, according to one of Trimble's key aides, said, 'Whatever you do, don't talk about fishing to Martin McGuinness or we'll be here all night.' Trimble's staffer said the remark appeared to reduce the tension in the room and lighten the atmosphere – the UUP delegation were as aware as Kelly of McGuinness's passion for fly fishing.

Manchester United was another passion of McGuinness's outside politics and in 2005 he sat down beside David Ervine at the funeral service for their mutual hero George Best in the Great Hall of Stormont.

In fact Trimble had always found it easier dealing with Martin McGuinness in the pre- and post-Good Friday Agreement negotiations than Gerry Adams. Reflecting on their very first bilateral meeting with the Sinn Féin leadership in 1998, ahead of the historic Holy Week that led to the Agreement, Trimble said, 'We find it easier to talk to Martin McGuinness than to Gerry Adams. Now McGuinness is short-tempered, but on the other hand he says something to you fairly straight, whereas in my opinion Adams is always playing games. Very frequently Adams is indirect in his language, while McGuinness is more direct. It doesn't mean I'm going to agree with McGuinness, but he is a bit more clear about where he stands.'

While Trimble and others might have been struck by the differences in personality between McGuinness and Adams, it is a fundamental fact that McGuinness and Adams worked in sustained partnership and were close friends ever since the Northern leadership seized power in the republican movement from the early 1980s onwards. The photographs in this book – from the nascent years of Sinn Féin's emergence as a serious political force after the 1981 hunger strike to the early peace process of the early 1990s – bear this out. Indeed, after Gerry Adams was shot and wounded in central Belfast by John 'Grugg' Gregg and other UDA members in 1984 the first port of call for Adams after his recovery was Martin McGuinness's home in Derry, en route to Donegal. One of Adams's security team at the time recalls driving Adams to the McGuinness household where he was warmly welcomed, 'as if the two men were brothers'.

That partnership was the core axis that kept the Sinn Féin peace project moving forward. There would have been no ceasefires, no end to the IRA's campaign and no decommissioning without both men working in tandem.

Despite numerous Ulster loyalist paramilitary plots to kill him, most notably by Michael Stone, McGuinness did not take a bullet for the cause. He also escaped long-term imprisonment. In terms of the Troubles, he was one of the great survivors. In the end the sixty-six-year-old died from a rare genetic disease. On Tuesday 21 March 2017 it was left to Adams to announce the death of his oldest and most trusted comrade. 'Martin, as we all know, was a very passionate Irish republican. He believed in our people – that people of this island should be free. He believed in reconciliation. He worked very, very hard at all of that,' Adams said. 'We are very, very sad that we lost him overnight.'

A few days later there was a poignant moment at the end of the funeral mass for Martin McGuinness inside Derry's Long Tower Church. As mourners – including prime ministers, ministers past, party leaders, old comrades, ex-enemies, friends and family – filed out of the church, Bill Clinton moved towards the coffin and said goodbye with a simple gesture: he lightly touched the coffin and smiled. This farewell was a symbolic act marking the end of McGuinness's astonishing journey; a final stop point in a political life that has helped shape the entire island of Ireland as we know it today.

Derry in the 1950s and a view of the Bogside. Even in the mid-twentieth century the nationalist Bogside, where Martin McGuinness was born in 1950, still resembled a city from the century before. It was in these narrow streets and huddled-up terrace houses that

McGuinness grew up, at a time when unionist power in the state appeared unassailable and the council's practice of gerrymandering and vote-rigging maintained an artificial loyalist majority on the local corporation. There was a strong localised Labourite tradition

in Derry; the city was also a bastion of moderate northern nationalism personified by Nationalist party MP Eddie McAteer (pictured here addressing a crowd at Meenan Park during the 1953 Stormont election campaign). He held the Foyle seat at Westminster up to 1969.

Derry's violent republican strain was a minor one within the wider nationalist electorate.

1

1950–1982

This first section of photographs deals with Derry, the city where Martin McGuinness grew up, and begins with the events of 1968 to 1972. Those four years see the emergence of the civil rights movement and the use of excessive force in response by the unionist government. The pictures capture the violence and brutality of the RUC and the British army and show how their actions trigger the wider Troubles. Peaceful protest turns into street disorder and finally into open armed insurrection.

Through these social seizures young men like McGuinness emerge, not just to 'pay back' the state for the oppressive way it policed the civil rights protests and later the slaughter on Bloody Sunday, but also to take up another more traditional battle: the struggle to end the partition of Ireland, which they undertook through the creation of a new IRA. What was meant to be, for many of the younger leftist idealists who led the civil rights campaign in the city, Derry's version of Paris '68 became an attempt by others to re-enact Dublin 1916 and the 'unfinished business' of the War of Independence – to violently unravel the Anglo-Irish Treaty of 1921.

The Stormont regime overnight loses the propaganda war after RUC officers are shown on television beating peaceful civil rights protestors in the streets of Derry. The baton-wielding policemen are breaking up a banned civil rights march in Derry on 5 October 1968 in the presence of Gerry Fitt MP and three British Labour MPs. The images are beamed across the world and remind viewers everywhere of the violent suppression of peaceful civil disobedience protests by black civil rights activists in the American Deep South. Two nights of rioting follow. The Northern Ireland government's response to civil rights demands – such as one man, one vote, and equality in jobs and housing – was to push a generation into the arms of more radical forces including, within a year, a newly formed Provisional IRA.

In August 1969 – with Catholic streets in Belfast burning in the wake of a loyalist backlash following the events in Derry – the British army is deployed in Northern Ireland. In those early days the troops are welcomed with tea and sandwiches and, to the horror of traditional republicans, are perceived as potential saviours of Belfast's Catholic population against a loyalist–Protestant onslaught. This so-called 'honeymoon' period is of course short-lived and, as these images of young Derry rioters demonstrate, just a month later, British soldiers are already seen as an occupying force. It is troops rather than RUC men and B-Specials who are now on the sharp end of the actions of what becomes the Derry Young Hooligan faction at Free Derry Corner. Out of this generation of anger-filled youth will emerge many of the cadre of the Provisional IRA's first recruits in the city.

British soldiers in Derry city on
Bloody Sunday.

The killing of thirteen unarmed Derry citizens on 30 January 1972 by the Parachute Regiment together with the introduction of internment without trial in August 1971 are the turning points of the early Troubles for the nationalist–Catholic community. IRA leaders reflecting on the massacre's impact said that within hours of the fatal shootings by the Parachute Regiment they could not cope with the numbers of young men and even young women queuing at their doors to sign up for the Provisionals.

© Stanley Matchett / victorpatterson.com

Father Edward Daly, later the Bishop of Derry, prays over one of the dead on the day that changed everything, not only for Derry, but for the whole of Northern Ireland.

Father Daly escorting one of those
wounded by British paratroopers
who had fired on unarmed civilians.

© Stanley Matchett / victorpatterson.com

St Mary's Church in the Creggan area
of Derry, 2 February 1972, where the
Requiem Mass for eleven of those killed
on Bloody Sunday was held .

One of the earliest portrait-style images of Martin McGuinness taken in May 1972, less than five months after Bloody Sunday. Although memories of Derry being part of all the '68 uprisings are fading fast, the fresh-faced redheaded young republican firebrand of this picture has a slight resemblance to one of the figureheads of the Paris student rebellion, the German '68-er revolutionary Danny Cohn-Bendit. By now McGuinness is already commander of the Provisional IRA in Derry while Cohn-Bendit ended up on a completely different path – the anarcho-libertarian was in the pacifist German Green Party by the 1980s.

The Keenans were one of the few families in Derry that kept the tradition of hardline, recalcitrant republicanism alive in a city where the main political struggle in the Bogside and other nationalist wards was between Labourites and the representatives of the old Nationalist Party. Here Martin McGuinness is pictured on 7 May 1972 alongside Seán Keenan Jnr, whose father Seán was one of the few stalwarts of the pre-Troubles IRA left in Derry.

Keenan Jnr, Phil O'Donnell, Keenan Snr and McGuinness pose together on the same May day. Both older men had recently been released from Long Kesh internment camp outside Belfast. They were among hundreds of people arrested and imprisoned without trial on 9 August 1971, accused of belonging to paramilitary organisations. Many of those detained in Operation Demetrius are not even involved in any faction of the IRA. Ironically many more who are interned belong to the Official IRA, whose leadership was at that time nudging its organisation in the north towards a more or less permanent ceasefire, which eventually came about on 30 May 1972.

The infamous side-on image of McGuinness pointing a Luger pistol on 6 May 1972 as part of a propaganda stunt by the Provisionals in Derry. The macho-militaristic pose was adopted to demonstrate to the world that, despite internment, the PIRA was still openly and brazenly able to organise in the city. A lifetime later in 2009, when Martin McGuinness was sharing power, the Traditional Unionist Voice hardliner Jim Allister asked this question: 'People were being slaughtered by the Provisionals around the time when this photo was taken. Was the gun which appears in this photo used in any of those attacks?'

Martin McGuinness's rise through the upper echelons of the Provisional IRA is evident in this image from 13 June 1972. He is present at the 'top table' of the Provos' high command alongside three of the organisation's founding fathers: Seán Mac Stíofáin, Dáithí Ó Connail and Seamus Twomey. They are also pictured (right) outside Derry's Brandywell Community Centre, the venue for the press conference.

At the press conference they outline the terms of a truce the Provisionals are offering the British government. Their proposals include a suspension of PIRA attacks for seven days in return for the British army ending searches, house raids and arrest operations. Another key demand is that a young – then unknown – republican called Gerry Adams be released from Long Kesh. Although the Conservative Northern Ireland Secretary William Whitelaw rejected the offer, he did agree to send a representative to meet the Provisionals' leadership at a secret location near Derry seven days later. The newly freed Adams joined Ó Connail to meet Frank Steele and Philip

© Derry Journal

© Mirrorpix

Woodfield, who represented Whitelaw at the talks.

The secret meeting in Derry led to high-powered talks between the Provisionals' national leadership and the British government at the late Tory minister Paul Channon's Cheyne Walk home in London the following month. McGuinness was one of the Provos' negotiators, along with Adams. The talks broke down with the British refusing to bend to IRA demands that they issue a declaration of intent to withdraw military forces. The PIRA's response, within forty-eight hours, was gun battles with the British army in West Belfast and, eventually, on 21 July, the Bloody Friday massacre in Belfast in which nine civilians died and over one hundred more were injured as twenty-six bombs exploded across the city. Following the breakdown of the Cheyne Walk talks McGuinness – reflecting on his eyeball-to-eyeball meeting with British cabinet ministers – said, 'I had learned in two hours what Irish politicians still haven't learned: that the British don't give in easily.'

From the slaughter of 1972 right up until 1976, each year was declared by the Provisionals as 'The Year of Victory'. In reality the Provisionals were settling in for the 'Long War'. McGuinness is pictured in a Garda minibus on 1 January 1973 being driven away from the non-jury court in central Dublin but he avoided a prison sentence in the Republic in spite of announcing in court: 'I am a member of Óglaigh na hÉireann and very, very proud of it.' Still only twenty-two, he was emerging as one of a group of northern-based IRA leaders who would reshape the Provisionals. McGuinness was to play a central role in creating the 'Northern Command' that would run the armed campaign from within Northern Ireland and that would also streamline the organisation into smaller, cell-like structures that were apparently harder for the security forces to penetrate.

© victorpatterson.com

In 1976 Martin McGuinness saw a lot of the courts system, north and south. Here he is on the morning of 2 March of that year leaving a Belfast court. This time he faced charges of IRA membership between 8 August 1973 and February 1976. After his arrest and time in custody he faced a full hearing that day. He gave an accomplished performance in the court, where he stated: 'I am a republican, but being a republican and a member of the IRA are two completely different things. I believe my arrest was a political move to get me out of the way. They were just holding me in cold storage.' He even told the court that all he wanted to do was go back to the Bogside and 'live quietly with my wife and child and mind my own business'. All charges of IRA membership were dropped after no evidence was offered against him.

© victorpatterson.com

© victorpatterson.com

In 1981, a number of republican prisoners at the Maze prison refused food with the aim of achieving the reintroduction of political status. This hunger strike was a game changer for McGuinness and Sinn Féin. Yet the only prisoners from his native Derry to die on the death fast, Patsy O'Hara and later Mickey Devine, both belonged to the smaller republican organisation, the Irish National Liberation Army. The INLA was a breakaway faction from the Official IRA. Activists like O'Hara were disillusioned over the 1972 ceasefire and formed a new organisation with an overtly leftist-Marxist tone to continue an armed struggle. O'Hara died after sixty-one days on hunger strike at the age of twenty-three. Although the INLA's political wing, the Irish Republican Socialist Party, organised O'Hara's funeral, many Sinn Féin and PIRA members filed behind the cortège in Derry. The irony was not lost on some INLA–IRSP Derry members, given that they believed Martin McGuinness had given the local IRA brigade orders to beat up O'Hara in the mid-1970s as part of a series of moves to intimidate and thus prevent the smaller, republican socialist movement from gaining ground in Derry.

The funeral of Bobby Sands, who was the first hunger striker to die and officer commanding of the IRA prisoners in the Maze, brought tens of thousands onto the streets of his native Twinbrook area of West Belfast. Sands had been elected MP for Fermanagh and South Tyrone in April 1981 after a by-election that followed the death of the previous MP, the independent nationalist Frank Maguire. Sands' victory convinced the IRA and Sinn Féin's high command that there was a potentially deep well of support within the nationalist electorate for their brand of republicanism. Indeed Gerry Adams himself wrote in *An Phoblacht* three years after the hunger strike that its main effect was to push the movement more rapidly towards electoral politics. For Adams it was 'easier to argue for an electoral strategy within republican ranks'. While Martin McGuinness willingly went along with Adams once it was obvious that Sinn Féin should enter the electoral fray, he had initially been slower to spot the potential of the prison hunger strike. He left the major running to Adams on the National H-Block/Armagh Committee, for instance, and was not as prominent in the campaign.

Martin McGuinness did, however, deliver the graveside oration in honour of an old friend from South Derry – Francis Hughes, the second IRA hunger striker to die. To McGuinness and republicans in both Derry city and county

Patsy O'Hara's funeral in Derry, 25 May 1981.

Hughes was a legendary 'operator'. In 1978, in a gun battle with police and troops during which a soldier was killed, Hughes initially escaped from the scene even though a large chunk of his thigh bone had been shot away. When he was later captured after hiding in thorn bushes Hughes was taken away on a stretcher still defiant, clenching his fists and shouting, 'Up the 'Ra!' In his speech at Hughes's grave, McGuinness told the thousands gathered around: 'His body lies here beside us but he lives in the little streets of Belfast; he lives in the Bogside; he lives in East Tyrone; he lives in Crossmaglen. He will always live in the hearts and minds of unconquerable Irish republicans in all these places. They could not break him. They will not break us.' To the unionist community, however, Hughes was a ruthless cold-hearted killer whose IRA unit in South Derry killed many people, including a nine-year-old girl who died when a booby-trap bomb planted underneath the family's car to murder her father exploded.

On the twenty-ninth anniversary of Hughes' death, McGuinness issued a statement about his old friend. 'Francis Hughes was one of the most fearless and formidable IRA Volunteers to emerge in this phase of the republican struggle ... Our struggle has changed greatly since the difficult summer of 1981 but we remain committed to our republican goals and we remain committed to delivering the sort of society which is demanded by the sacrifice of hunger strikers like Francis Hughes.'

OPPOSITE: Bobby Sands's funeral, 7 May 1981.

ABOVE: Francis Hughes's funeral in Bellaghy, 15 May 1981.

2
1982–1998

This press conference in 1982 is the launch of Sinn Féin's campaign for the elections for a new Northern Ireland Assembly. McGuinness is seated beside Adams; both wearing the tweed jackets that seem to have been ubiquitous among Sinn Féin politicians in the early '80s. The slogans on the election posters are worth noting: 'Break the British Connection' and 'Smash Stormont'.

Sinn Féin won five seats in these elections, with McGuinness and Adams elected in Derry and West Belfast respectively, but the party would boycott the Assembly and all attempts to restore devolution at this time. Yet this image of an all-male cast that looks more like a gathering of university or polytechnic lecturers than the republican movement's leadership is still one of the first milestones on the party's long road towards solely peaceful politics. The hunger strike and the election of Sands, and other prisoners in the Irish Republic to the Dáil, in that preceding highly charged summer did open the way for Sinn Féin to participate seriously in elections. A couple of decades later McGuinness was no longer saying that Stormont should be smashed – but was instead working within the devolved system, first as education minister and later as deputy first minister.

The pictures in this section span the period of Sinn Féin's first serious steps into electoral politics in Northern Ireland whilst at the same time reflecting the ongoing violence raging all around. The trail of coffins, the graveside orations, the confrontations with RUC riot squad units in cemeteries, the men in masks in the cortèges all seem like an unending procession of misery from which there is no escape. Yet within a decade the imagery alters radically and the section ends with McGuinness within the corridors of power – in Washington DC, inside the Houses of Parliament or outside 10 Downing Street – looking visibly more relaxed and genial.

Martin McGuinness in Derry in May 1983,
a month before the general election.

Election posters for Martin McGuinness go up in Derry as he contests the Westminster seat of Foyle for the first time in 1983. He polls a respectable 10,607 votes but is more than 13,000 behind John Hume. It will take Sinn Féin thirty-four years to wrestle the seat away from the SDLP.

© Derry Journal

The early to mid-1980s and McGuinness appears as caught up in republican funerals as he is engaged in Sinn Féin's political struggle. We see him here laying the Irish tricolour across the coffin of Eamon 'Bronco' Bradley, whose death at the hands of British troops in Derry's Racecourse Road in 1982 is a source of controversy in the city to this day. There have been calls for public inquiries into the fatal shooting three decades on.

After failing to threaten Hume and the SDLP's hegemony in Derry in the 1983 election, McGuinness had to turn to other urgent political matters. These included dealing with the fallout from the British government banning Martin Galvin, Noraid's publicity director,

from entering Northern Ireland. Noraid was the original fundraising arm for the PIRA in North America. As well as raising money for prisoners and their families, and mounting pickets against British policies, Noraid also smuggled guns to the IRA.

In August 1984, as these images on the right show, Galvin defied the ban and came to Derry, and was photographed with McGuinness at the memorial to Bradley.

His presence in Belfast later in the same month caused even more controversy. RUC officers moved in to arrest Galvin on the Andersonstown Road in the west of the city, and one was caught on camera firing a plastic bullet into the chest of Sean Downes,

who later died as a result of his injuries.

McGuinness and Galvin would later fall out over Sinn Féin's peace strategy, in particular the party's agreement to a set of principles laid down by another American citizen – US senator George Mitchell – a year before the 1998 Good Friday Agreement. While the McGuinness–Adams double act eventually persuaded Sinn Féin and the IRA to embrace the Mitchell principles, a recalcitrant minority broke away to form the Real IRA. They included Bobby Sands' brother-in-law Michael McKevitt. Galvin supported McKevitt's view that the Mitchell principles on non-violence undermined the IRA's historic 'right' to wage armed struggle to end partition.

© Pacemaker Press International

© Derry Journal

© Derry Journal

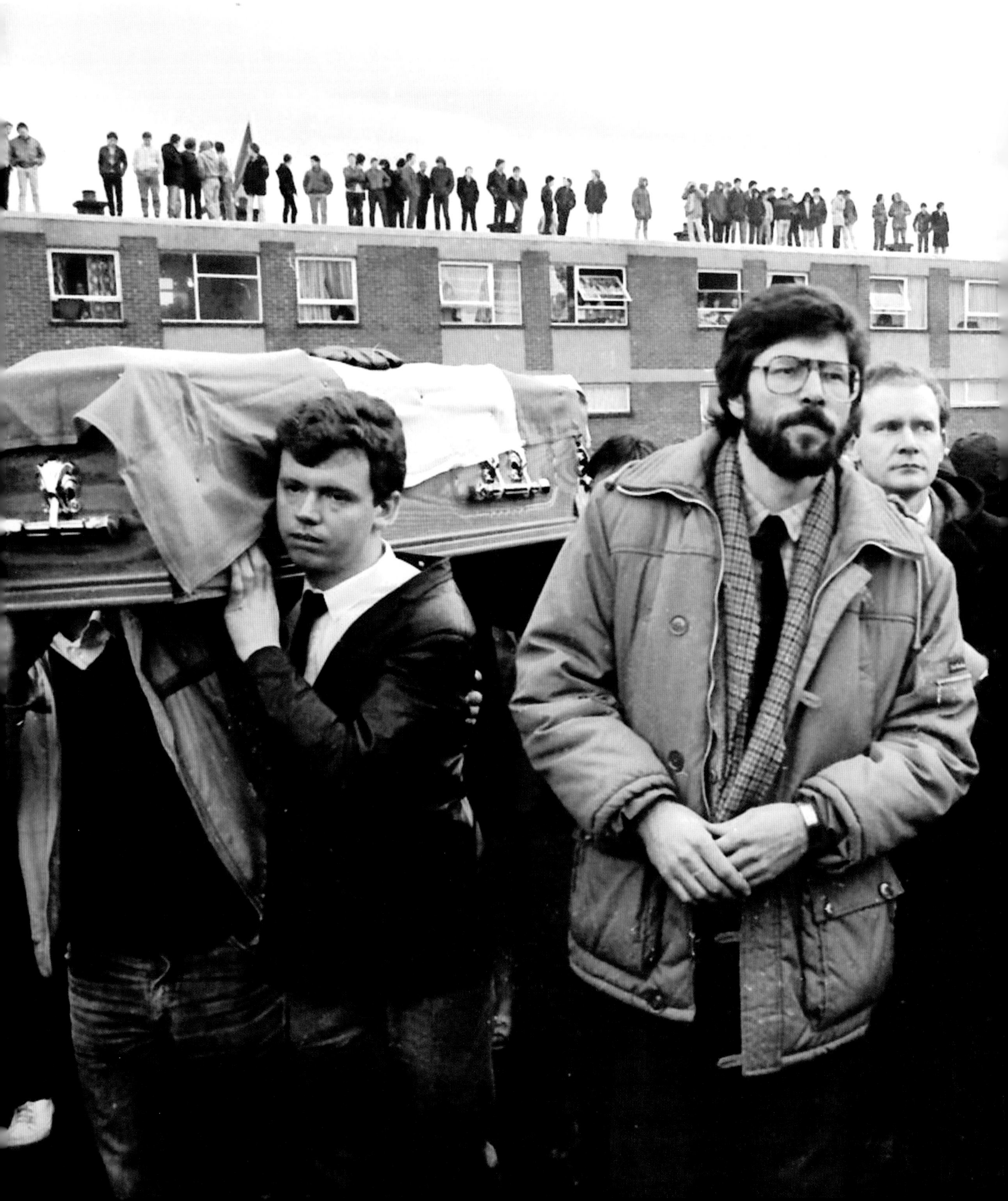

© Derry Journal

The coffins of Derry Brigade IRA members William Fleming and Danny Doherty being carried through Derry in December 1984. The pair had driven to Gransha Hospital to kill a man they believed to be a part-time member of the Ulster Defence Regiment. However an SAS unit was lying in wait. McGuinness later claimed Fleming was hit thirty-eight times in the SAS ambush while Doherty was shot thirty times. Delivering the graveside oration, McGuinness said that 'only the freedom fighters of the IRA could bring Britain to the negotiating table'.

Martin McGuinness is seen here remonstrating with an RUC officer at the funeral of IRA man Henry Hogan in Dunloy, County Antrim, in February 1984. Hogan was killed in a gun battle with undercover soldiers, one of whom also died. McGuinness is telling the police inspector to get his officers out of the church grounds. At the time the RUC had adopted a policy of preventing any shows of paramilitary strength at funerals – such as masked men flanking the coffin or firing parties letting off shots over the grave – as had been commonplace during the 1981 hunger strikes. The inevitable outcome of this policy was a series of violent stand-offs and riots at the funerals of IRA members.

© Pacemaker Press International

Martin McGuinness in Belfast for the funeral of IRA member Sean McIlvenna who was shot dead at the scene of a landmine explosion directed at a UDR military patrol in 1984, in which seven UDR men were injured, two of them seriously. Sinn Féin's publicity director Danny Morrison is directly to McGuinness's left with Gerry Adams at the edge.

© Pacemaker Press International

Seamus McElwaine was a legendary IRA gunman to republicans in the border counties of Tyrone and Fermanagh; to unionists he was a ruthless murderer. McElwaine was shot dead by the SAS on 26 April 1986. Martin McGuinness delivered the address at McElwaine's graveside and told mourners that the IRA activist was a 'freedom fighter murdered by a British terrorist'.

Arlene Foster believed it was McElwaine who shot and gravely wounded her policeman father at their family farm a few years earlier. She later described McElwaine as a 'sectarian killer' who was 'behind the murder and attempted murder of many Protestants along the Fermanagh border'.

© Derek Speirs

Martin McGuinness and Gerry Adams are joined at the top table by Danny Morrison at the 1985 Sinn Féin Ard Fheis. This is just one year before the annual congress at which McGuinness and Adams finally get their way, and force an end to the policy of abstaining from the Dáil. This is made easier by the fact that in 1985 McGuinness is elevated to the post of IRA northern commander, the year that also brings a subtle change in Sinn Féin's attitude towards the SDLP, with Adams making his first call on John Hume for a pan-nationalist approach to the north.

The funeral of Charles English, who died when a home-made grenade exploded in the vehicle in which he was travelling while on an IRA operation in August 1985.

Four years before, James English, Charles English's brother, had been killed along with another Derry teenager when they were struck by a British army Land Rover.

In the period between December 1984 and April 1985 thirteen IRA members were killed on active service; nine of them shot dead by the SAS.

McGuinness files behind the coffin.

McGuinness carries the coffin with his brother Willie.

In the streets of the Bogside in
November 1985.

At Sinn Féin's Republican Information
Centre in Derry in 1986, with the famous
poster of Bobby Sands beside him.

© Kaveh Kasemi / Getty Images

At one of the early wave of republican wall murals – this one off the Falls Road in Belfast had gone up during the Hunger Strike. At the very end of 1985, shortly after this picture was taken, McGuinness was held for seven days at the RUC's Castlereagh interrogation centre in East Belfast. He was questioned about the murder of Kurt Konig, a 38-year-old Catholic caterer originally from Germany, who was shot dead by the IRA in Derry. Konig had been targeted because he was supplying catering services to the RUC. During his incarceration in Castlereagh, according to veteran RUC officers, McGuinness never said a word.

At the Bloody Sunday commemoration in January 1986 Martin McGuinness is seated beside guest speaker, the Labour Leader of the Greater London Council, and future Mayor of London, Ken Livingstone. The latter's presence caused huge controversy back in Britain even though Livingstone had previously been to Belfast to meet with McGuinness and Adams four years earlier. Livingstone had travelled across because the then Home Secretary Willie Whitelaw banned McGuinness and Adams from travelling to London where they were to be Livingstone's guests.

At the time, McGuinness, Adams and the republican leadership invested great faith in Livingstone and the likes of Tony Benn on Labour's far left. They believed that Thatcherism's hegemony could not last and that a British electorate, fed up with mass unemployment and the harshness of monetarism, would put a left-wing Labour government into office – a Labour party whose leftist factions promised to pull British troops out of Northern Ireland. A year later, of course, Margaret Thatcher won another landslide victory in the 1987 general election, giving the Tories a hat-trick of electoral triumphs.

The violence in the north sometimes spilled onto the streets of Dublin, such as in 1986, when Gardaí fired shots following the release from court of IRA suspect Evelyn Glenholmes. The Belfast woman had just walked free on a technicality – the authorities had spelt her name incorrectly on the extradition warrants. At the time she was wanted in connection with a number of IRA atrocities in Britain including the bombing of Harrods. Gardaí tried to rearrest her as she walked up Prince's Street North towards O'Connell Street with shots being fired close to what was then British Home Stores on Dublin's main thoroughfare.

At Derry's Guildhall Martin McGuinness is seated just behind Eamonn McCann, the civil rights activist, socialist and journalist. Despite their differences on many issues – most notably McCann's critique of the efficacy of the IRA's campaign of violence – the pair did share platforms when it came to controversies like media censorship of Sinn Féin spokespersons or the supergrass system, as well as other socio-economic issues in the city.

Larry Marley was a senior Provisional who helped mastermind the IRA's breakout from the Maze in 1983. He was shot dead on 2 April 1987 after loyalist gunmen from the Ulster Volunteer Force smashed into his home in the Ardoyne district of North Belfast. The subsequent funeral for this PIRA icon turned into a major test of the RUC's policy of preventing paramilitary shows of strength. There was a heavy police presence outside the Marley home and the funeral was held up for several days as RUC riot squad officers sought to prevent any paramilitary displays as Marley's remains were carried out of the door. At one stage the coffin was laid on the ground outside his home by mourners who refused to leave until the police pulled back. The stand-off was violent, fractious and bitter.

© Mike Abrahams / Alamy Stock Photo

© Pacemaker Press International

ABOVE: Mourners and RUC officers outside Marley's home.

RIGHT: McGuinness appeals to the RUC riot squad to pull back outside the Marley home. Bottom left is a moustachioed man, growling at the police lines. This is Freddie Scappaticci, who at this time was the IRA's chief spy catcher, heading up an internal security unit that tracked down, interrogated and killed informers within the organisation. Unknown to all those republican mourners around him, Scappaticci was, arguably, the British state's most important spy inside the IRA. Scappaticci, incidentally, had a particular antipathy towards McGuinness.

ABOVE: McGuinness remonstrates with the RUC on the second day of the deadlock.

RIGHT: A mass protest in Ardoyne against the RUC's actions.

The funerals of Mairéad Farrell, Seán Savage and Daniel McCann – the IRA members shot dead by the SAS in Gibraltar on 6 March 1988. The trio had been planning, alongside another female IRA activist, to place a bomb at a military cemetery targeting British troops. McGuinness was among the thousands of mourners marching behind their coffins in West Belfast ten days later.

© Richard Moore

LEFT: McGuinness and Adams by the grave in Milltown cemetery.

BELOW: There is a visible reaction in the crowd as the first grenades explode.

The funeral of the Gibraltar Three at Milltown cemetery became a televised terrorist attack. Michael Stone threw grenades and fired shots into the crowd, killing three people, including an IRA activist from West Belfast, and injuring more than fifty. The UDA-aligned killer from East Belfast had a particular animus against McGuinness. Later, after he was convicted and sent to the Maze prison, Stone regretted not killing either McGuinness or Adams, of whom he said, 'I decided I was going to blow them away.' A new hate figure, of course, for nationalists and republicans, Stone became at the same time an inspiration to a generation of new hard-line young loyalists. Johnny 'Mad Dog' Adair claimed that Stone's solo run at Milltown convinced him to sign up to the UDA's murder squad, the Ulster Freedom Fighters.

The killings at Milltown mark the start of an upsurge in loyalist paramilitary violence. By the early 1990s, the loyalists are killing more people than the IRA, putting further pressure on the republican movement as well as the general nationalist population.

© Chris Steele-Perkins / Magnum Photos

Mourners stream between the graves
at Milltown cemetery.

The aftermath of the attack, showing a clearly shaken McGuinness with victims of the attack, and holding up Michael Stone's gloves and bullets.

Father Alec Reid administers the last rites to David Howes, one of the two British army corporals who were captured and killed when their unmarked car drove into the cortège of the funeral of Caoimhín Mac Brádaigh, one of the victims of Michael Stone's attack at Milltown. The photograph encapsulates the horror of 1988 when there apppeared to be no end to the conflict.

© Pacemaker Press International

ABOVE: 1991 is the year of two landmark commemorations – the twentieth anniversary of internment without trial and the tenth of the Maze hunger strike. McGuinness is the key speaker at the rally to remember both events in West Belfast.

RIGHT: In August 1993 Sinn Féin breaks new ground by organising its first mass rally through Belfast city centre to City Hall. Party activists carry an enormous Irish tricolour through the streets of central Belfast and surprisingly the loyalist response, at least in the city centre, is muted.

Frizzell's fish shop was destroyed by an IRA bomb on Saturday 23 October 1993. The Provisionals' leadership in Belfast had plotted to kill the UDA's ruling body – the inner council, including Johnny Adair – that met frequently in a room above the fish shop. Adair and the UDA command were not actually in the room above the premises that fateful Saturday. Instead, the IRA bomb placed by Thomas 'Bootsey' Begley and Sean Kelly killed nine Protestant civilians, including two children. Begley also died in the explosion. Gerry Adams was reported to be 'incandescent with rage' following the IRA's botched, disastrous and bloody operation. Martin McGuinness may well have thought the same, given that at exactly this time he was deeply involved in secret talks based on The Link, a clandestine network of contacts that included McGuinness, the former priest Denis Bradley, and MI5 and MI6 officers. Publicly, Adams took most of the flak in the aftermath of the Shankill Bomb disaster. He carried Begley's coffin.

© PA Archive / PA Images

The gaping hole on Belfast's Shankill Road where Frizzell's fish shop used to be.

TOP: The clear-up operation following the explosion.

BOTTOM: The funeral procession for Thomas Begley, travelling from his Ardoyne home to Milltown cemetery.

McGuinness had additional troubles of his own to deal with in 1993. Here he is pictured at the Sinn Féin advice centre in Derry the day after ITV's investigative programme *The Cook Report* described him as the most dangerous man in Britain. Among the many allegations in the programme was the claim by the family of Frank Hegarty that McGuinness had lured the IRA informer back to Derry. He had allegedly promised Hegarty's elderly mother that her son would be safe if he returned and admitted to his treachery. Another damning element was taped testimony from a republican colleague about McGuinness's leading role in the IRA. The voice on the tape belongs to the man who stood just a few feet away from McGuinness at the Larry Marley funeral back in 1987 – Freddie Scappaticci, aka Stakeknife.

TIME FOR PEACE
25 YEARS
- TIME TO GO -

Despite the Shankill Bomb, the loyalist retaliation at Greysteel a week later – in which eight people were killed by the UDA – and the waves of violence and counter-violence of 1993, McGuinness and Adams managed to keep nudging the Provisionals towards a ceasefire. Here they appear on a platform outside Sinn Féin's West Belfast headquarters, Connolly House, on 31 August 1994, the day the IRA declared a total cessation of violence.

© Martin McCullough / PA Archive / PA Images

© Pacemaker Press International

TOP: Hundreds turn out on the Andersonstown Road in what is clearly a carefully organised demonstration of joy, relief and triumph. There are cavalcades of Falls Road taxis with republican supporters hanging out of them, waving flags, punching the air and giving V for victory signs.

BOTTOM: The partnership on which the Provisionals' peace strategy rested – Martin McGuinness and Gerry Adams – proudly march through West Belfast on the same historic day. Among those at the pair's side is veteran North Belfast IRA man Terence 'Cleeky' Clarke (on Adams's right).

While republican supporters tried to portray the ceasefire as a victory, the *Belfast Telegraph*'s headline was probably a more accurate reflection of the relief that most people in Northern Ireland felt on that day: 'After 3,168 deaths and 25 years of terror, the IRA says ... IT'S OVER.'

At the 1986 Sinn Féin Ard Fheis, as part of McGuinness's and Adams's attempt to secure the delegates' support for the dropping of the policy of abstentionism in relation to the Dáil, McGuinness issued this promise from the platform of Dublin's Mansion House: 'Our position is clear and it will never, never, never change. The war against the British must continue until freedom is achieved.' Yet the IRA 'war' had ended less than a decade after that bellicose speech, without a British withdrawal or even a statement of the intent.

© Crispin Rodwell

A young boy in Belfast leaps into the air while playing handball against a mural. It is 31 August 1994 – the day the Provisional IRA declared its ceasefire. The image represents a society looking forward in hope.

ABOVE: In 1995, one year after the IRA ceasefire, Martin McGuinness is in the Palace of Westminster asking the Labour party in particular to back Sinn Féin's entry to talks, even in the absence of decommissioning. He is sitting beside Jeremy Corbyn, MP for Islington North and future Labour leader, one of Sinn Féin's most loyal allies in the British parliament.

LEFT: During the press conference in parliament's Jubilee Room McGuinness rules out the decommissioning of any weapons as a means of breaking the deadlock in the peace process in Northern Ireland, saying that the IRA would see any such move as an act of surrender.

This photographs shows the extent of the destruction caused by the IRA bomb which ripped through the heart of London's Canary Wharf district on 9 February 1996. The explosion marked the end of the IRA's 1994 ceasefire. The bomb killed two men, injured more than a hundred others and caused more than £100 million worth of damage. The blast left a vast crater, and was felt all across east and northeast London.

The political reverberations were massive, of course, although the Adams–McGuinness leadership almost immediately put in place a strategy to try and distance themselves from responsibility for the ceasefire breakdown. The pair, echoing the IRA statement, sought to blame John Major and his government for stalling on moves to convene all-party talks including Sinn Féin, as well as London's (and unionists') demand for the decommissioning of paramilitary weapons.

© Associated Press

With the IRA back in conflict mode once more – with further bomb attacks in Britain including the devastation of part of central Manchester on 15 June 1996, where over 200 people were injured – Sinn Féin are locked out of the political negotiations at Stormont. Here Martin McGuinness talks to a man behind the wire, an unnamed Northern Ireland Office official, at Castle Buildings on the Stormont estate in June 1996. McGuinness had led the Sinn Féin delegation to the talks from which they were now excluded. He and Sinn Féin would remain shut out of the talks until a second IRA ceasefire was declared in the summer of 1997.

McGuinness holds up a plastic baton round during a rally on 12 July 1996. It had been one of the most turbulent climaxes to the Ulster loyalist marching season, with disturbances all over Northern Ireland, from Drumcree in Portadown to Belfast, Dunloy and Derry. An estimated nine hundred petrol bombs and other missiles were fired at RUC and army lines in McGuinness's native city, and dozens of plastic bullets were fired at rioters. Forty-one civilians and eleven police officers are injured in Derry alone. The violent atmosphere in the city and beyond did not augur well for any resumption of the ceasefire.

Nor behind the political machinations did the picture appear favourable for McGuinness and Adams in the IRA leadership. Both men were re-elected to the army council at an IRA convention that summer but a majority on the Provisionals' ruling body had put a harder line in place – there would be no more cessations of violence unless there was a British declaration of intent to withdraw from Northern Ireland.

© Pacemaker Press International

McGuinness has just come out of Omagh Leisure Centre after being elected MP for the constituency of Mid Ulster in May 1997, the year of Tony Blair's landslide election victory. The man who announced that McGuinness had secured 20,294 votes – just a couple of thousand ahead of the Democratic Unionist Party's Reverend William McCrea who had held the seat since 1983 – was the very same election official who confirmed that hunger striker Bobby Sands had won the 1981 Fermanagh and South Tyrone by-election.

McGuinness had carefully and quite deftly sold himself to the constituency as the man who could bring the IRA back to a ceasefire. The strategy clearly worked: middle class nationalist voters deserted the SDLP and 'lent' Sinn Féin their votes to strengthen McGuinness's hand within the wider republican movement. Some SDLP figures bitterly quipped that it was a strategy of 'vote for us or we'll shoot'. They were soon to discover that what happened in Mid Ulster was not a temporary phenomenon: thousands upon thousands of nationalists shifted their allegiance to Sinn Féin once a second ceasefire was in place.

© Pacemaker Press International

A rare public outing for Martin McGuinness's two sons, Fiachra and Emmett, as they enjoy their father's electoral triumph in Mid Ulster.

© PA Archive / PA Images

© PA Archive / PA Images

Gerry Adams pictured among republican supporters on Belfast's Falls Road after Sinn Féin's surge in the 1997 general election. His victory in West Belfast was particularly significant as he had previously lost that seat to the SDLP's Joe Hendron in 1992. The hands of the key duo pushing the Provisionals towards a purely peaceful path within the movement had been doubly strengthened.

Throughout the violent, often bloody, hiatus between the 1994 and 1997 ceasefires the Sinn Féin leadership sought to identify John Major as the main stumbling block on the road to political progress in Northern Ireland. The triumphant entry of Tony Blair into 10 Downing Street marked a major sea change in British politics. Although secret talks continued between British officials and the republican leadership through the ceasefire-breach period, McGuinness and Adams saw Blair as a British politician they might be able to do business with, given both his commanding majority in the House of Commons and his apparent willingness to shake things up.

Martin McGuinness goes to Westminster on 13 May 1997. The new MP for Mid Ulster is pictured outside the Houses of Parliament as he adheres to the Sinn Féin policy of boycotting the Commons. In fact, McGuinness was in London to visit Róisín McAliskey in Holloway Prison. The pregnant prisoner, daughter of civil rights icon Bernadette Devlin McAliskey, had been mooted as an alternative republican candidate in the Mid Ulster constituency. Her mother had been acidic in her assessment of the IRA ceasefire, reflecting at the time of the first cessation that 'the good guys had lost'. Róisín McAliskey, however, was dissuaded from standing against McGuinness; if she had not been, the republican–nationalist vote would have been split. Out of gratitude, McGuinness visited her in jail and campaigned for her release.

He also used his trip to London to press his claim for office space inside Westminster, even though he would not sit on the Commons' green benches. Speaker of the House of Commons Betty Boothroyd hastily introduced new rules denying facilities to MPs who refused to take up their seats.

© Associated Press

The McGuinness–Adams duo in action outside Westminster on 19 May 1997. The pair refused to swear the oath of allegiance to the queen which all MPs must do before taking up their seats. Intriguingly, both got invited to speak by left-wing veteran Labour MP Tony Benn, using a loophole that would allow them to say something as the Commons elects a new speaker, before the oath is sworn. But McGuinness and Adams turned down Benn's offer, fearing criticism at home from within the republican rank and file, and, more critically, from the men on the Provisional army council whom they had to win over for another ceasefire.

Gerry Adams announces the restoration of the IRA ceasefire on 19 July 1997. A month earlier Martin McGuinness had received a crucial piece of information from the Northern Ireland Office: that if the ceasefire were restored, Sinn Féin would be welcomed into the talks by the end of July. Both he and Adams had to attend a series of IRA army council and IRA executive meetings throughout July to argue the case for a second cessation.

Their argument was that Sinn Féin's vote was increasing, a new government was in place in London that promised the party entry into political negotiations, and the combined weight of the recently elected Fianna Fáil-led government in Dublin alongside Bill Clinton in the White House would work favourably for Irish republican interests in the forthcoming talks.

A confident Martin McGuinness, wearing the green ribbon in support of IRA prisoners incarcerated in jails across Britain and Ireland, leads a powerful Sinn Féin delegation into talks at Stormont to meet Mo Mowlam. Despite her decision to force 'Orange feet' down Portadown's Garvaghy Road, McGuinness and Mowlam strike up a warm relationship over the course of negotiations. Adams, of course, is by McGuinness's side, as is Martin Ferris, the Kerry-based former IRA gunrunner, and Lucilita Bhreatnach. The three men pictured here on 6 August 1997 had been named the previous weekend by an Irish government minister as belonging to the IRA's ruling army council. By now the British government has laid down the target date of 15 September for all-inclusive talks to begin, with Sinn Féin now inside the tent.

Fast forward to 29 January 1998 and Tony Blair makes a commitment in the House of Commons to hold an inquiry into the events of Bloody Sunday in Derry twenty-six years earlier. It had been a key demand made by Martin McGuinness as part of a series of confidence-building measures to keep republican faith in the peace process. The inquiry, chaired by Lord Saville, would eventually hear testimony from McGuinness himself and others, including the IRA informer-exile Willie Carlin, confirming that Sinn Féin's chief negotiator in the peace process had been the Provisionals' deputy commander in the city on the day of the atrocity.

6 September 1997 sees Martin
McGuinness at Dublin Airport, alongside
Gerry Adams and recently elected Sinn
Féin TD to the Dáil, Caoimhghín Ó Caoláin,
who has topped the poll in the June Irish
General Election for the constituency
of Cavan–Monaghan. The trio are on
their way to Washington DC to meet Bill
Clinton's security adviser Sandy Berger.

On Capitol Hill the three Sinn Féin politicians are pictured with influential US Senators Chris Dodd (between McGuinness and Adams) and Ted Kennedy. McGuinness has another agenda while in the United States: after this photograph and a dinner for the trio at Washington's Waldorf Astoria hotel, he flies out to California. Mindful of the IRA base back at home, McGuinness visits three republican prisoners who escaped in the mass Maze jail breakout of 1983, and three other ex-IRA men living illegally in the United States. All six face extradition from the United States back to Britain.

Back in Ireland on 9 September 1997, Sinn Féin sign up to a set of rules allowing them to enter the all-party talks in Belfast. The talks are named after US Senator George Mitchell, the independent chairman of the negotiations that lead to the Good Friday Agreement the following year. Signing the six Mitchell Principles – which include a commitment to pursuing political goals through purely peaceful means and, critically, commit parties to the 'total disarmament of all paramilitary organisations' – is a watershed moment for Sinn Féin and indeed the IRA. The initial impact of Sinn Féin agreeing to the Mitchell Principles is that the US Department of Justice, on the advice of Secretary of State Madeleine Albright, drops extradition charges against the six Irish republicans. Albright's intervention comes about after advice from Martin McGuinness that this would advance the peace process.

Martin McGuinness takes centre stage outside 10 Downing Street on 11 December 1997. To McGuinness's left are Lucilita Bhreatnach, Martin Ferris, Gerry Adams and the Sinn Féin president's long-time press officer, Richard McAuley. To his right, he is flanked by future Sinn Féin Fermanagh and South Tyrone MP Michelle Gildernew and the late Siobhán O'Hanlon. The latter was there as a note-taker for the IRA army council, a job she was tasked with during the early negotiations with the NIO, Mowlam and the British prime minister. O'Hanlon was trusted because of her IRA activist credentials. A niece of IRA veteran and longstanding Adams–McGuinness ally Joe Cahill, O'Hanlon was a convicted bomber, who was named in some reports as the fourth member of the IRA cell in Gibraltar in 1988, although she denied it.

In late 1997, by the time O'Hanlon reported back to the IRA's supreme decision-making body, the McGuinness–Adams axis had just survived an attempted coup d'état by hard-liners the previous month. A mixture of luck and cunning had enabled the pair to face down a challenge by the then IRA quartermaster general, Michael McKevitt, over the signing of the Mitchell Principles. McKevitt had argued at an IRA army convention in County Donegal in November that adhering to the principles abandoned a key tenet of the republican movement's ideology: the historic 'right' to wage war until partition was ended and a united Ireland was achieved. McKevitt skulked off to form a new recalcitrant violent dissident republican group – the Real IRA. It was an organisation that would end up at odds with Martin McGuinness, and would later cause him to do the once unthinkable: to publicly denounce acts of republican violence.

McGuinness, alongside Gerry Adams, leads the Sinn Féin delegation into the negotiations at Castle Buildings in Stormont on 23 March 1998. Between the two men is Bairbre de Brún, who would later take up one of Sinn Féin's two cabinet seats in the first post-Good Friday power-sharing administration as minister for health, social services and public safety. The party is back at the talks following a fortnight's suspension over allegations of ongoing IRA activities.

© Associated Press

Adams checks his watch as he goes out on one of his private walks-and-talks with McGuinness around the grounds of Castle Buildings on 7 April 1998. During the weeks building towards Good Friday and the agreement the pair are regularly seen out together, away from the other parties. The duo probably suspected that their office in the building where the discussions took place was bugged. Around the time of this picture the talks were on a knife-edge, with unionist negotiators including David Trimble extremely wary of what the talks chair, Senator George Mitchell, was putting on the table.

On 10 April 1998 George Mitchell holds the first copy of the Good Friday Agreement, signed by all the parties represented at the talks, with the exception of the Democratic Unionists.

Bertie Ahern had buried his mother two days earlier and had come straight back from her funeral to the negotiations. Ahern and Tony Blair look visibly relieved that a deal has finally been reached.

3

1998–2017

This final section is a two-decade sweep through the tumultuous and at times personally challenging events that shaped Martin McGuinness's legacy. It's an arc that covers the Good Friday Agreement; the Omagh bomb explosion; McGuinness's initial taste of ministerial power as head of education in the first devolved government at Stormont; the forging of a remarkable friendship with the Reverend Ian Paisley; the report of the Saville Inquiry into Bloody Sunday; the functioning of a partnership government for almost ten years; and, eventually, his death and funeral in his native Derry.

Perhaps the most striking aspect of this section is how happy and relaxed McGuinness appears to be, particularly within the Chuckle Brothers period, when he and Paisley were in the top jobs as first and deputy first ministers. There are a few profoundly dark spots in this timeline, such as the destruction and carnage in Omagh. However, most of these images have a lightness that contrasts sharply with the gritty, black-and-white imagery from the earlier sections, especially the photographs from the worst days of the Troubles. That contrast, both in terms of film–light quality and content–context, tells us all we need to know about the transformation of Martin McGuinness.

Martin McGuinness and Gerry Adams on Good Friday 1998, wearing their Easter lilies to remember the 1916 Rising. Naturally, their badges are held on with a pin – in the 1969–1970 split, the Provisional IRA reverted to using the traditional paper-and-pin Easter lily, while the Officials used a self-adhesive backing, hence the nickname 'the Stickies'.

At a packed special Sinn Féin Ard Fheis in Dublin's RDS conference centre on 18 April 1998, McGuinness and Adams share a few words at the top table. The pair are about to persuade the party faithful to endorse the Good Friday Agreement. The Agreement, however, has also to be endorsed by a much bigger electorate – the voters of the Irish Republic and, most crucially, those of Northern Ireland. The referendum on the Agreement is to take place a month later on 22 May.

In fact an event at this Ard Fheis hands those arguing for a 'no' vote – Ian Paisley's DUP and Robert McCartney's UK Unionist Party – a major propaganda weapon. Tony Blair agreed to give temporary release to four IRA members for the event. Labelled the Balcombe Street Gang after the siege in the London thoroughfare where they surrendered after taking hostages, they were jailed in the mid-1970s for six hundred years between them for a series of bomb attacks and other atrocities in England. They are paraded in front of Sinn Féin delegates, whom they urge to back the McGuinness–Adams leadership and support the Good Friday Agreement, and are feted like heroes. However, the sight of convicted killers let out on temporary leave for politically expedient reasons sickens many wavering voters within the unionist community. Paisley and McCartney portray the early freedom for the gang responsible for thirty-five deaths in England as the shape of things to come for the Northern Ireland public – with the release of more paramilitary prisoners, including mass murderers, forming part of the peace deal.

© Alan Lewis / Stringer / Getty Images

Intriguingly, during his speech to the Ard Fheis, Adams urges delegates to 'keep an open mind' at the end of the party's two-day debate on the Agreement. As ever, when Adams and McGuinness are singing from the same hymn sheet, the delegates swing their way. It is interesting to recall, however, that when it came to the actual heavy lifting during the referendum campaign, Sinn Féin's slick, mass organisation on the ground is not as active in urging a 'yes' vote within the northern nationalist community as, say, the SDLP.

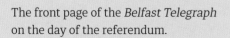

The front page of the *Belfast Telegraph* on the day of the referendum.

Not everyone within the fractious factions of Irish republicanism agrees that the Good Friday Agreement creates a pathway to the ultimate goal of a united Ireland. McGuinness and Adams feature in a cartoon with Mo Mowlam hovering above them as a group called 'Gerry and the Peacemakers', who are on a 'sell-out tour of Ireland'. The poster represents the view of the republican dissidents who broke away from the IRA and Sinn Féin mainstream following the split in 1997. The message is crystal clear – McGuinness and Adams have abandoned traditional values in favour of a newly resurrected Stormont. Or, as the SDLP deputy leader and soon-to-be deputy first minister, Seamus Mallon, later remarks, the pair have accepted 'Sunningdale for slow learners' – a reference to the 1974 power-sharing agreement which the provisionals opposed and loyalist extremists pulled down. McGuinness's old nemesis from Derry, the Irish Republican Socialist Party, are one of the few republican organisations to campaign openly for a 'no' vote in the referendum.

Gerry Adams and Martin McGuinness sign the register document before entering the Assembly Talks at Castle Buildings, Stormont, on 10 July 1998. It has been a frenetic few months for them and all the other politicians. The two Sinn Féin leaders correctly gauged the mood of the nationalist electorate in Northern Ireland, especially in relation to the May referendum. Despite allegations of selling out and treachery from a range of republican hardline groups, ranging from Republican Sinn Féin to the IRSP, an estimated 97 per cent of Catholics/ nationalists in Northern Ireland voted Yes, as did a far smaller majority of the Protestant/unionist community – around 51 to 53 per cent. Overall, just over 71 per cent of Northern Ireland voters backed the Agreement. The vote clearly strengthens the McGuinness–Adams line inside mainstream republicanism.

Just twelve months before this photograph was taken, republicans and nationalists had chanted 'no ceasefire, no ceasefire' when the RUC and British army forcibly removed them from the Garvaghy Road in Portadown to make way for the Orange Order. McGuinness visits in July 1998 to make it clear that Sinn Féin stands by the nationalist residents who this year have had the Orange Order parade banned from going down their road.

The ban, however, leads to some of the worst violence associated with the Drumcree stand-off. It only ends after a series of sectarian attacks on vulnerable Catholic families in other parts of Northern Ireland, including in Ballymoney, County Antrim, where Richard, Mark and Jason Quinn (aged 11, 9 and 7) died when their home was petrol bombed. The RUC said that the children, whose mother was Catholic, were the victims of a sectarian attack. The triple murder is denounced by religious and political leaders, both Protestant and Catholic, and creates serious fissures within the Orange Order.

After weeks of street disorder the region pulls back from the brink once more.

The aftermath of the explosion in Omagh, County Tyrone, on Saturday 15 August 1998. The huge car bomb kills twenty-nine men, women and children, including a woman pregnant with twins. More than two hundred people are injured – many of them rushed to the small, over-run local hospital on pub tables, transported via a fleet of buses. By late afternoon the hospital is home to scenes that call to mind a war zone, with military helicopters landing in fields around it to ferry the most seriously wounded victims to larger hospitals in Belfast. The attack is carried out by the Real IRA whose origins lie in the split within the Provisionals the previous year. It is the deadliest single bombing in the history of the Troubles and comes only a few months after the hope and promise of the Good Friday Agreement, the May referendum and the election of a 108-strong Assembly. No one has ever been convicted in a criminal court in connection with the atrocity, although a successful civil action later taken by the families of some of the Omagh victims 'names and shames' alleged Real IRA leaders in court.

The Sunday papers on 16 August 1998 are full of headlines that reflect the carnage and massacre. As the body count rises and the backgrounds of the victims are established, it becomes clear that those killed, or in some cases horrifically maimed, are from a mix of faiths and origins, and include local Protestants and Catholics alongside children on holiday from Spain. Up until that day, which the *Mail on Sunday* calls 'Bloody Saturday', the Real IRA had been engaged in a campaign of car bomb and mortar bomb attacks aimed at destabilising Northern Ireland, and preventing a political settlement between unionism and nationalism. Before the Omagh bomb, however, their geographical targets had been mainly Protestant-unionist dominated towns, such as Banbridge or Portadown.

The following day Martin McGuinness and Gerry Adams arrive at Omagh's leisure centre which has been turned into an 'information clearing house' for families trying to find out if their loved ones were caught in the explosion. Many arriving at the centre have come back from summer holidays or weekend breaks across the border in places like County Donegal. There are very distressing scenes as people discover the names of the dead and injured on print-outs stuck to the walls of the centre. McGuinness and Adams had just returned from meeting with Tony Blair and Bertie Ahern. Speaking to reporters McGuinness denounces the attack by former comrades as 'indefensible' and predicts that the nationalist–republican population will pile pressure on the Real IRA to call off its campaign.

Secretary of State for Northern Ireland, Mo Mowlam, in Omagh on the following Monday morning signing the book of condolence for the victims and their families. It is the start of a week during which prime ministers and even a US president come to the Tyrone town to pay their respects. McGuinness and Adams are under pressure, not only to condemn the bombing, but also to call for nationalist cooperation to help catch those responsible for the atrocity.

Martin McGuinness takes his place in the first power-sharing cabinet since 1974. He holds the education portfolio for Sinn Féin in the multi-party coalition, and Bairbre de Brún is minister for health, social services and public safety. There are two ministers missing from the cabinet table – Nigel Dodds and Peter Robinson, who refuse to sit in the same ministerial room as McGuinness and de Brún. However, the two DUP ministers take an à la carte approach to their own portfolios – declining to sit around the cabinet table but still running their respective departments.

A beaming McGuinness tries out his new ministerial desk at the Department of Education's headquarters at Rathgael House for the first time on 30 November 1999. His core policy in office is to abolish the eleven plus transfer test.

© Pacemaker Press International

Back to where it all began on 6 December 1999 when McGuinness visits his old primary school, St Eugene's in Derry. This is his first visit to a school since his nomination as education minister. On his first day in office there were a handful of walk-outs and protests by some Protestant schoolchildren in places such as East Belfast but, in general, the demonstrations are few and far between.

McGuinness attends a protest against loyalist paramiliary violence in central Belfast on 18 January 2002, one of many rallies held across Northern Ireland that day following the sectarian killing of Royal Mail worker Danny McColgan in Rathcoole, North Belfast. A unit of the Ulster Defence Association is responsible for the murder of the young postman as well as a series of other sectarian attacks in the north of the city over this period.

© Sion Touhig / Getty Images

McGuinness is confronted by Victor Barker whose young son James was one of the victims of the Real IRA Omagh bombing in 1998. Barker accuses him here – as he has done on several occasions – of not doing enough to urge the republican community to inform on those behind the bomb. Barker claimed McGuinness was more concerned with maintaining an omertà over the role of former comrades in the bombing than helping to catch his son's killers. McGuinness, however, repeats that he utterly condemns the Real IRA, the organisation responsible for the explosion.

Martin McGuinness met Victor Barker as he walked with Gerry Adams to the Palace of Westminster on 21 January 2002. Sinn Féin would take up offices inside parliament but, thanks to a deal forged by Tony Blair, the party's MPs would not have to take the oath of allegiance - a former condition. It meant that although McGuinness still refused to sit in the House of Commons, his staff were now able to run their political operation in the parliamentary buildings.

The disagreements over IRA disarmament coupled with Sinn Féin's refusal to support policing and justice in Northern Ireland led to the collapse of the Executive in 2002. A year later there was a new scenario, following the 2003 Assembly elections in which the DUP had become the largest party. Now Ian Paisley was where he had always wanted to be – leader of the biggest unionist party. Paisley's former legal adviser, QC Desmond Boal, is said by one former Ulster Unionist to have been asked why his old friend finally entered government with McGuinness. Boal answered by recalling a conversation he allegedly had with Paisley a few years into the peace process, prior to the

Belfast Agreement. He had asked Paisley if he could ever foresee a time when he would share power with republicans, to which Paisley replied, 'Only when I am on top!'

The 2003 elections also marked a turning point for Sinn Féin. The SDLP, which had until then been the leading nationalist party, lost a significant number of seats. Sinn Féin, on the other hand, made substantial gains, with the result that, for the first time, they had the same number of seats in the Assembly as the SDLP.

However it took three more years for devolution to be restored. The intensive, multi-party talks at St Andrews led to a breakthrough and the agreement

of the same name. A year earlier John de Chastelain, the retired Canadian general, responsible for overseeing the decommissioning process since 1997, announced that the vast majority of the IRA's weaponry had been 'put beyond use'. McGuinness described the act of decommissioning in 2005 as helping to 'bring the final chapter on the issue' of the IRA's weapons.

'Of course, this is about more than arms. It is about reviving the peace process, it is about the future of Ireland,' he said. 'I believe that Ireland stands on the cusp of a truly historic advance, and I hope that people across the island will respond positively in the time ahead.'

© Associated Press

© Associated Press

By now Adams and McGuinness are under sustained pressure to nudge Sinn Féin and the republican movement towards the final act that will create a once-unthinkable power-sharing arrangement with, of all people, Ian Paisley and his Democratic Unionist Party. That act is to accept the full legitimacy of the Police Service of Northern Ireland, and to recognise the courts and judicial system within the region. This is a core DUP demand before entering a devolved government with Sinn Féin and it is one that has the complete backing of the Bush administration in Washington DC, and in particular, of the president's special envoy, Mitchell Reiss.

© AFP / Stringer / Getty Images

The era of the Chuckle Brothers has arrived! All beams and smiles now between newly sworn in Deputy First Minister Martin McGuinness and First Minister Ian Paisley on 8 May 2007. Paisley talks about 'a real chance for lasting peace' on the steps of the Great Hall inside the Stormont Parliament Buildings. The start of the McGuinness–Paisley era is akin to the end of the movie *Casablanca* when Humphrey Bogart turns to Claude Rains and says, 'Louis, I think this is the beginning of a beautiful friendship.'

© Charles McQuillan / Pacemaker Press International

And the laughter between the two men just doesn't stop. Even the EU's José Manuel Barroso gets the giggles on 1 May 2007 at a press conference in Stormont's Parliament Buildings. The EU commissioner was in Belfast to announce fresh European support through its peace-funding schemes to help economically bolster the McGuinness–Paisley led power-sharing government.

McGuinness and Paisley on the bridge of a Stena Line HSS vessel to mark the opening of a new ferry terminal in Belfast on 4 June 2008. Also on board is Scotland's First Minister, Alex Salmond.

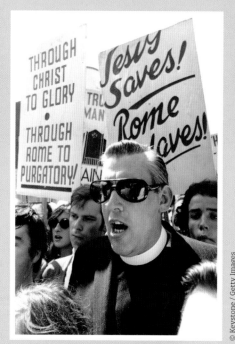

Two images from Paisley's past. One is of a younger firebrand preacher warning about the dangers of the Protestant churches' 1960s 'détente' with the Roman Catholic church. The other is from the mid-1980s and the pan-unionist protests against the Anglo-Irish Agreement of 1985, which, it should be noted, Martin McGuinness, Sinn Féin and the Provisional IRA also opposed.

Touché! Paisley's sledgehammer has been replaced with a cricket bat or two. McGuinness and Paisley joke about with two cricket bats on 12 July 2007. The pair are at Stormont to welcome home Irish cricket heroes Trent Johnston, team captain, and Kyle McCallan, spin bowler. Ireland's exploits at the Cricket World Cup that summer included an unprecedented and unexpected win over Pakistan. Despite cricket being a quintessentially 'English gift' to its former colonies Martin McGuinness was a self-confessed cricket fan. He once told the *Guardian* about his love for the game which stretched back to the 1960s: 'I thought it was really interesting. It was a game where discipline was required. An intriguing battle between bowler and batsman. I became very interested in the different techniques and strategies that were deployed around it.' Some of his former comrades expressed surprise

over his love of cricket but, McGuinness continued, 'over the years I've learned that other Irish republicans have a great interest in all sorts of sports, including cricket. Raymond McCartney, a former hunger striker, is also a fan.'

When Ian Paisley died on 12 September 2014 Martin McGuinness initially reacted to the news with a comment on Twitter: 'I have lost a friend.' Later McGuinness remarked, 'Over a number of decades we were political opponents and held very different views on many, many issues but the one thing we were absolutely united on was the principle that our people were better able to govern themselves than any British government. I want to pay tribute to and comment on the work he did in the latter days of his political life in building agreement and leading unionism into a new accommodation with republicans and nationalists.'

Another Irish republican who was interested in cricket, albeit as a means more of knowing thine enemy, was the convicted IRA bomber, arms smuggler and supposedly ideologically hard-line Brian Keenan. The Belfast republican once told the late IRA informer Sean O'Callaghan while the pair were incarcerated in a prison in Britain, 'Don't trust the English – they invented cricket!' This meant perhaps that Keenan feared that the British knew how to play a long game when it came to the business of counter-insurgency. McGuinness and Adams took key roles at his funeral, to pay their respects to a dead comrade but also to express their thanks for Keenan's support for their strategy at critical points of the peace process, particularly around the time of the 1997 Real IRA split. 'He was central to securing the support of the IRA leadership and rank and file for a whole series of historic initiatives,' said Adams.

For several years before his death Keenan had been portrayed as the dangerous ideologue who could at any time bring down the McGuinness–Adams plan. In fact Keenan, who once negotiated secret arms deals with both Libya and Syria, proved in the end to be a loyal and faithful servant to the strategy. He played a critical role in preventing the nucleus of what was to become the Real IRA leadership from overthrowing McGuinness and Adams on the army council during the summer and autumn of 1997 in the internal republican battle over the Mitchell principles.

McGuinness unfolds the Irish tricolour over Keenan's coffin on 24 May 2008. The sixty-six-year-old had died earlier that week after a battle with cancer.

McGuinness and Adams carry the coffin
from Keenan's West Belfast home.

At the graveside of an IRA veteran executed by the Irish Free State in the 1940s, Brian Keenan said that the only thing that would ever be decommissioned was 'the British state in Ireland'. One wonders not only what he made of the decommissioning of IRA weapons, and the recognition and support of the PSNI, but also what he would have thought of Martin McGuinness's forthright condemnation of republican violence by 2009. On 10 March of that year McGuinness joined the new First Minister of Northern Ireland Peter Robinson and the PSNI's first Chief Constable Sir Hugh Orde outside Stormont Castle. It had been a bloody weekend in Northern Ireland

with two British soldiers and a PSNI officer killed by republican dissidents. The upsurge in dissident republican violence posed a major threat to the fragile power-sharing arrangement. Yet McGuinness incurred the hard-liners' wrath by denouncing the killers as 'traitors to the island of Ireland', who he said had 'betrayed the political desires, hopes and aspirations of all of the people who live on this island'.

The comments are, in terms of Irish republicanism, a crossing of the Rubicon for Martin McGuinness, and one not without danger. Ruairí Ó'Brádaigh, McGuinness's old nemesis whom he and Adams effectively deposed from the republican leadership back in 1983,

zeroed in a week later in an interview with the *Observer* on McGuinness's use of the word 'traitors' to describe the armed republican dissidents behind the three killings that March. 'When I heard it, I thought immediately "Who is the traitor?" Is it those who just behave as they always behaved and believe sincerely as they always believed in republican struggle? Or are they the people who turned their coats like McGuinness, accepted British rule, destroyed the arms, who said they would never accept a unionist veto and now have done so? In my view, McGuinness has abused words,' Ó'Brádaigh remarked.

McGuinness knew his comments would provoke some former comrades, even in his native city. On 24 April 2009 he turns up at the murals on the Bogside in a public act of defiance against the republican dissidents. He holds a press conference in the street close to Free Derry Corner to reveal death threats made against him by anti-ceasefire republicans. His presence on the Bogside that afternoon wins him widespread sympathy as well as admiration throughout the nationalist community and indeed far beyond.

Commentators sought to contrast the warmth of the relationship McGuinness had forged with Paisley with the colder, more businesslike modus operandi between the deputy first minister and Robinson. In reality the affinity between the two men was much greater than the public realised. The pair often talked about football, with McGuinness being a Manchester United fan and Robinson a lifelong follower of Chelsea. Perhaps the most public manifestation of that close relationship came in 2010 when Robinson faced the worst personal and political crisis of his life – the revelation that his wife and fellow DUP MP Iris Robinson was having an affair with a younger man for whom she secured a £50,000 loan from some of the party's financial backers. Among the few to show support and sympathy for the Robinsons was Martin McGuinness. He appealed for privacy and space for the Robinsons to sort out their personal difficulties, and appeared genuinely concerned for the entire family.

A year later McGuinness attended the funeral of Iris Robinson's mother, ninety-year-old Marie Duffield Malloy, to show solidarity again with the beleaguered first family of Northern Ireland. McGuinness would also display open affection for Iris Robinson when they met in Dublin at another historic event a few years later.

LEFT: Martin McGuinness and Peter Robinson at a joint press conference at Hillsborough Castle, 5 February 2010.

ABOVE: McGuinness and Robinson wait on the steps of Stormont Castle to meet Irish Foreign Minister Micheál Martin on 11 November 2009.

© Oli Scarff / Getty Images

Thousands on the march from the Bogside to Derry's Guildhall Square on 15 June 2010 as the families get ready to hear the final verdict of the Saville Inquiry into Bloody Sunday. The inquiry, which cost in excess of £191 million and lasted for twelve years, finally exonerates those who were shot dead by the Parachute Regiment as innocent victims. Here the marchers pass a mural remembering that fateful civil rights march, which ended with carnage on the streets and left a lasting, bitter legacy – one that helped give propulsion to the Provisional IRA's armed campaign.

Martin McGuinness with Kay Duddy, sister of Jackie Duddy, one of the thirteen shot dead by Paratroopers on 30 January 1972, while on the walk towards Guildhall Square. A giant television screen has been erected to beam Prime Minister David Cameron's speech live from the House of Commons into the square.

Cameron issues a formal, state apology for the 'unjustified and unjustifiable' killing of civilians in Derry on Bloody Sunday. The five-thousand-page, ten-volume report concludes that there was no justification for shooting at any of those killed or wounded on the march: 'None of the firing by the Support Company [Paratroopers] was aimed at people posing a threat or causing death or serious injury.'

Cameron adds in his statement to MPs: 'The government is ultimately responsible for the conduct of the armed forces, and for that, on behalf of the government and on behalf of the country, I am deeply sorry.' The declaration of innocence and the unqualified apology produces wild applause and cheering among the crowd in Guildhall Square.

© Colm Lenaghan / Pacemaker

John Kelly celebrates on 15 June 2010. His brother Michael was one of the victims of Bloody Sunday.

© Derry Journal

Former US president Bill Clinton with Peter Robinson, Martin McGuinness and John Hume on 29 September 2010 just before he makes a speech at Magee College in Derry. It is Clinton's first visit to the city since his trip to Northern Ireland in 1995. In these new optimistic times Clinton later tells his university audience that politicians like McGuinness and Robinson need to 'finish the job' on issues such as dealing with the legacy of the past. Clinton reminds the nearly thousand people in attendance that the examples of McGuinness, Robinson and Hume have 'inspired the world' and given hope to other societies locked in conflict. His visit comes just a week ahead of the first and deputy first ministers' trip to the United States, where they will attend a major international economic summit.

© Charles McQuillan / Pacemaker Press International

Clinton beside McGuinness on the platform, the two men having become good friends during the course of the peace process. Although the crowds are down on the throng of twenty-five thousand that flocked to see Clinton at the Guildhall Square event five years earlier, the former president still commands respect for his ongoing engagement in Northern Ireland affairs.

© Pacemaker Press International

© Charles McQuillan / Pacemaker Press International

© Stephen Barnes / Politicians / Alamy Stock Photo

Darren Clarke's victory at the 2011 Open Championship made him the second Northern Irish golfer in just four weeks to win a major golf tournament after Rory McIlroy won the US Open in June of the same year. The deputy first minister said that over the four days of the US Open Clarke had 'conducted himself with a grace and quiet determination that is nothing short of outstanding'. In return, Darren Clarke backs the Northern Ireland Executive's call for the Open tournament to be hosted in one of the region's top golf resorts.

September 2011 and Reverend David Latimer, minister at First Derry Presbyterian, attends the Sinn Féin Ard Fheis. He is the first Protestant clergyman to address Sinn Féin delegates at their annual congress, which – in another first – is held in Belfast, at the city's Waterfront Hall. In his speech Latimer describes Martin McGuinness as 'one of the great leaders of modern times'.

Speaking directly to McGuinness, the Presbyterian minister says: 'Martin, you and I have been journeying together for the last five years, and in that time we have become very firm friends able to relax in each other's company ... While our interaction might understandably raise eyebrows amongst some within our communities, the reality is you and I regard ourselves to be brothers within the same human frailty. Your invitation to me is forward-looking and timely – is it possible that the Democratic Unionists could see their way to invite a Catholic priest to address their party conference this year or next?'

In 2013, Father Tim Bartlett was on a panel at the DUP party conference.

Martin McGuinness is one of seven candidates vying to be the next president of Ireland in 2011. Here his image is draped over Sinn Féin's headquarters in Dublin's Parnell Square. It is a particularly bruising and difficult campaign for McGuinness to fight, and a lesson that politics south of the border are wholly different from the political battles of Northern Ireland. In one live televised debate the veteran journalist Vincent Browne challenges McGuinness on his membership of the Provisional IRA and when exactly he left the organisation. McGuinness claims he left PIRA after 1974 but this is disputed by Browne who then produces eight books on modern Irish republicanism, including McGuinness's unofficial biography co-written by Kathryn Johnston and the late Liam Clarke, which state that he remained central to the organisation right up to and beyond the peace process.

On the campaign trail there are other challenging moments, none more so than when the son of an Irish Army private shot dead by the IRA in 1983 confronts McGuinness about his father's death. Private Patrick Kelly and Garda Gary Sheehan were killed during a shoot-out between the Irish security forces and the IRA unit that had kidnapped millionaire businessman Don Tidey.

Holding up a picture of his father Patrick, David Kelly says, 'I want justice for my father. I believe you know the names of the killers of my father and I want you to tell me who they are. You were on the army council of the IRA.' On the stump in Athlone, McGuinness is visibly floored and replies, 'I don't know their names.' The incident reminds many voters about McGuinness's IRA past, especially when David Kelly retorts, 'He [Patrick Kelly] was loyal to this Irish Republic and I am loyal to him as a son and I want justice for him. I want justice for my father and I want your comrades who committed this crime to hand themselves in to the Gardaí.'

© Derek Speirs

© Derek Speirs

The entire McGuinness family is photographed with the would-be president. For many years McGuinness, for wholly understandable reasons, kept his family out of the limelight.

© Derek Speirs

At the campaign launch with Gerry Adams. Adams is now fully embedded in southern Irish politics as TD for Louth and the party's leader in Dáil Éireann. McGuinness's candidacy attracts international media attention given his history and reputation. His presence enlivens what could have been a lacklustre, forgettable presidential race. However, despite his global fame, McGuinness comes third in the election. The Labour candidate – former minister, Galway TD and poet Michael D. Higgins – wins 701,101 first preference votes, nearly 40 per cent of the vote; the independent senator Seán Gallagher gets 504,964 or almost 29 per cent, and McGuinness obtains 243,030 first preferences; just under 14 per cent.

2011 has been a busy year politically for the Irish Republic. The country elects a Fine Gael–Labour coalition to power,

sweeping aside Fianna Fáil, whose ministers, after three previous election victories, are blamed for the collapse of the Celtic Tiger and then the national humiliation of the state being bailed out from bankruptcy by the International Monetary Fund and the European Central Bank. Sinn Féin's vote surges and they return with fourteen seats in the Dáil, their best-ever performance in an Irish general election.

It is also the year that Barack Obama visits Ireland and discovers the roots of his Irish ancestors in Moneygall. Prior to President Obama there was another important visitor – Queen Elizabeth II. She wins over the Irish populace with her laying of a wreath to remember all the dead of Ireland's struggle for independence at the Garden of Remembrance in Dublin. Her speech at Dublin Castle containing Gaelic

references, and later her walkabout in the English Market in Cork are regarded as a high point in twenty-first-century Anglo-Irish relations. Although Sinn Féin does not take part in the protests against the British royal visit, the party declines invitations from the Irish state to attend the various events surrounding the queen's first-ever historic tour of the Republic. With sharpened political antennae and a nose for what way public opinion in nationalist Ireland is swaying, McGuinness realises that the party may have missed an opportunity to rebrand itself in the eyes of the southern Irish electorate. He will ensure they do not make the same mistake again. Indeed he presages a future meeting with the queen during the 2011 presidential campaign when he says that if elected head of state he will meet all his counterparts, including Elizabeth II.

In June the following year the historic handshake finally happens inside Belfast's Lyric Theatre, which the queen visits to mark its re-opening. On BBC Radio 4's *Today* programme McGuinness subsequently explains that part of his motivation for meeting and shaking hands with the queen was to 'extend a hand of friendship, peace and reconciliation' to unionist people.

That handshake in the Lyric Theatre, with Peter Robinson looking on approvingly, was the first of many encounters with the British monarch. Two years later at a banquet in London that the queen has hosted to welcome President Higgins to the UK, McGuinness remarks that the woman he used to refer to as Mrs Windsor is now playing a 'leadership role' in the peace process. McGuinness says he believes the queen is a 'staunch supporter' of the Irish peace process who had impressed him with her words and deeds during her highly symbolic state visit to the Republic of Ireland in May 2011. This remark, on 6 April 2014, is the strongest evidence that McGuinness regarded Sinn Féin's boycott of the queen's visit to Ireland three years earlier as a tactical mistake.

McGuinness later claimed that his three meetings with the queen, including the first one in Belfast, put him in danger. A year after attending the London banquet McGuinness said police had told him that the Continuity IRA had planned to assassinate him when he was travelling by using a rocket launcher. In a defiant message to the CIRA, McGuinness said, 'I will not be silenced or deterred. These people are only interested in plunging us back into the past. If those behind this threat think they have the ability to destroy the peace agreements, which have been endorsed by the overwhelming majority of the people of Ireland, then they are clearly detached from reality. They need to wise up, listen to the people of Ireland and abandon these futile actions.'

Martin McGuinness speaks at the Tim Parry Jonathan Ball Peace Foundation's twentieth-anniversary Peace Lecture. The charity was set up to remember the two young boys, aged twelve and three respectively, who were killed by two IRA bombs in the Lancashire town of Warrington in February 1993. Ahead of his lecture to the foundation McGuinness takes part in a press conference with Colin Parry, the father of one of the murdered boys. McGuinness describes the Warrington bomb, which provoked anti-IRA protests by thousands in Dublin, as a 'shameful act'. Colin Parry did face some criticism from groups representing IRA victims for inviting McGuinness to deliver the lecture but defended the invititation on the grounds that it would further foster peace in Northern Ireland.

Speaking about a demonstration outside the event by Justice 4 the 21 – a campaign group for victims of the IRA's Birmingham pub bombings in 1974 – Parry said: 'I understand [the protestors] because we met in private and had an open and difficult conversation, but the protestors should respect the founding principle of why we built this foundation, which was we would work in areas of peace building and reconciliation. And you can't be an active player in that arena unless you have an open-door policy.'

McGuinness revealed that he learnt about the Warrington explosion while waiting for a secret meeting with British government representatives aimed ultimately at securing an IRA ceasefire. Outlining the moral complexities of the peace process of the early 1990s, McGuinness recalled: 'I was involved in trying to build bridges to the British government and was in the process of trying to organise a meeting with a major representative of the government. The meeting was to have happened that Saturday [of the bombing]. It didn't take place, but it did take place two days later in Derry, and it's been a remarkable journey.'

Martin McGuinness is the main speaker at Sinn Féin's own 1916 Easter Rising centenary commemoration outside Dublin's General Post Office. Speaking from the platform in O'Connell Street on 24 April 2016, McGuinness tells thousands of Sinn Féin members and supporters that theirs is the only party committed to achieving Irish unity. Referring to the 1916 Proclamation read out at the GPO by rebel leader Patrick Pearse one hundred years earlier, McGuinness tells the gathering that the 'mission statement' of the Proclamation was far ahead of its time, offering equality, democracy and social justice when the world knew very little at that time about these ideas. McGuinness uses the occasion to criticise the largest political parties, particularly Fine Gael and Fianna Fáil, whom he labels the 'self-serving political parties' of the 'establishment', claiming they had all stood by during times of crisis for Irish republicanism. 'Sinn Féin is the only political party on this island working to end that fracture in their nation and to achieving the republic set out in the Proclamation,' McGuinness said.

© Derek Speirs

McGuinness shares a joke with Gerry Adams as they walk along O'Connell Street towards the party commemoration. A few years before they had spoken about the centenary being a target date for Irish unity. By the time the anniversary arrived, though, such talk had been quietly dropped. McGuinness's unionist partners in government meantime boycotted the anniversary of the Rising. The 2016 Easter commemoration is a reality check for modern Irish republicanism – when the Good Friday Agreement was signed in 1998 even media commentators in Belfast, let alone Martin McGuinness and other Sinn Féin luminaries, were confidently predicting that a United Ireland would be in place within two decades.

© Derek Speirs

The deputy first minister is a guest at the Irish government's official 1916 Easter Rising centenary celebrations on 27 March 2016. The Fine Gael minority coalition backed by the main opposition party Fianna Fáil has decided to put the official army of the state – the Irish Defence Forces – at the centre of its centenary commemorations. The three-hour ceremony and parade by about four thousand members of the Irish army, navy and air force as well as Gardaí and the emergency services was heavy with historical resonance and peppered with rich ironies. Perhaps the most ironic of all was the sight of Martin McGuinness on one of the VIP platforms, sitting close to fellow northerner and former president of Ireland Mary McAleese.

Martin McGuinness was seen applauding the Irish military personnel, including veterans from fifty years of UN peacekeeping service as they marched past – even though the Provisional IRA he played such a pivotal role in claimed to be the sole true inheritors of the 1916 rebels during the Troubles, and the only legitimate Irish armed force. McGuinness and his comrades once even referred contemptuously to the official Irish military as 'Free State forces'. Indeed those same 'Free State forces' helped incarcerate many of his Derry Brigade comrades throughout the Troubles.

The tone and content of the speeches at the official state ceremony were in sharp contrast to the large Sinn Féin demonstration later in April. The message from the official commemoration was encapsulated by a prayer of remembrance for all the dead of the Rising delivered by Father Séamus Madigan, head chaplain to the forces. The prayer outside the General Post Office was also as much about the present in Northern Ireland as the past. 'Together, on this island, we have achieved a new peace. We cherish that peace, as we cherish all of the children of this island equally. We pray for all those who have suffered in the Troubles of the past century, and we hope for peace and reconciliation in the century that stretches before us.' Praying for 'the people of Ireland, from all traditions, at home and abroad,' Madigan said Ireland was now singing a new song of 'compassion, inclusion and engagement'. It is fair to say that the Martin McGuinness of 2016 would have had little problem with the sentiments expressed in that prayer. Indeed it could be argued that, had he have lived longer, McGuinness would have been a stronger voice than those that came after him in securing a compromise between Sinn Féin and the DUP at Stormont.

Deputy First Minister McGuinness holds a press conference with the new First Minister of Northern Ireland Arlene Foster on 19 May 2016. The relationship will never be as warm as the one McGuinness enjoyed with Ian Paisley, or indeed with Peter Robinson. Foster has long-standing reasons to be wary of Irish republicans. Her policeman father was almost killed by the IRA in the Troubles. She nearly lost her own life in an IRA bomb attack on her school bus, the Provisionals' target being the driver who was a part-time member of the security forces. Fermanagh-born Foster, like so many Protestants and unionists in the frontier constituencies, regarded themselves for decades as a people under siege and under attack from IRA units that could easily slip across the border into relative safety in the Irish Republic.

© Colm Lenaghan / Pacemaker Press International

On the steps at Stormont with Prime Minister Theresa May, who became leader of the Tory Party after David Cameron gambled and lost in the Brexit referendum of June 2016. This visit, a month after the referendum, was May's first visit to the region since entering 10 Downing Street. May had something in common with McGuinness – both were on the Remain side in the EU referendum whilst Foster and the DUP were firmly in favour of leaving Europe. Yet within a year of this picture being taken May would be required to ask for Foster's support to prop up her own government in Westminster. Like Cameron on Brexit, May gambled with an earlier-than-expected general election, which backfired on her and the Tories.

© Irish Eye / Alamy Stock Photo

McGuinness and Foster wait on the steps of Stormont Castle on 3 November 2016 for the arrival of Colombian President Juan Manuel Santos Calderón. He has travelled to Northern Ireland as part of a fact-finding mission, with the aim of helping him and his government in Bogotá to negotiate a ceasefire with FARC, the main insurgent leftist guerrilla force in Colombia.

The relationship between the two Northern Irish leaders is increasingly fractious. The crisis over a renewable heating scheme that Foster and the DUP once championed is about to blow up into a damaging scandal. Indeed, by the new year, McGuinness resigns as deputy first minister in protest over Foster's refusal to temporarily stand down while an independent inquiry is held into the Renewable Heating Incentive. Under the complex rules of power sharing, his resignation means there is no cross-community support for the Northern Ireland Executive to rule the region – the devolved government of almost a decade collapses.

© Colm Lenaghan / Pacemaker Press International

The haunting image of Martin McGuinness after he is driven away following his resignation as deputy first minister on 9 January 2017. It is a poignant photograph of a man who by now knows that he is seriously ill and facing death. Even political foes express their concern over the state of his health.

Relations between the two main parties of unionism and nationalism in Northern Ireland deteriorate rapidly, especially without McGuinness there to help smooth things out. The force of personality and the impact of the individual cannot be underestimated in politics – least of all in the Irish context.

© Colm Lenaghan / Pacemaker Press International

One of McGuinness's last public acts is to hand over the reins of power in Sinn Féin – at least in the north – to Michelle O'Neill. Here he is announcing O'Neill as the party leader in the Assembly on the steps of the Stormont on Monday 23 January 2017. Among those looking on is Sinn Féin's National Chairman, Declan Kearney (on the right, wearing a red tie). Obscured slightly by McGuinness is the man many had tipped to be northern leader instead, the former minister and one-time MP for Newry and Armagh, Conor Murphy.

Martin McGuinness's sons carry their father's coffin home on 21 March 2017, draped with a tricolour, the rain pouring down on Derry. It marks the start of several days of mourning during which world leaders will mingle with friends, neighbours and comrades of Martin McGuinness, all wanting to say their farewells. The sixty-six-year-old had died, surrounded by his family, in Derry's Altnagelvin hospital. In the immediate aftermath of his death, world leaders paid tribute to the man who had transformed from firebrand revolutionary to peacemaker. Buckingham Palace confirmed on the same day that the queen would send a private message of condolence to McGuinness's widow, Bernie.

© George Sweeney / Alamy Stock Photo

The old and the new generations of mainstream republicanism carry McGuinness's coffin on the day of his funeral, 23 March 2017. Behind is his old friend and key ally for more than thirty years, Gerry Adams. At the front is Michelle O'Neill who received McGuinness's blessing as the new northern Sinn Féin leader just a couple of weeks earlier. McGuinness is being carried through the streets of the Bogside where he grew up, where he led the Derry Brigade of the Provisional IRA, and where he had held secret talks with British envoys in the Derry 'Link' that eventually produced the peace process. The funeral passed by iconic wall murals that marked key events from the early Troubles, such as the 1969 Battle of the Bogside and Bloody Sunday.

© Derek Speirs

Within hours of McGuinness's death on 21 March 2017, the family of the late Ian Paisley sent warm messages. Kyle Paisley, a Free Presbyterian minister like his father, tweets on learning of McGuinness's death: 'Very sorry to hear about the passing of Martin McGuinness. Look back with pleasure on the remarkable year he and my father spent in office together and the great good they did together. Will never forget his ongoing care for my father in his ill health.'

Kyle Paisley's younger brother and North Antrim MP Ian Junior later remarks that McGuinness had been on a 'remarkable journey that not only saved lives but made the lives of countless people better'. Their mother, Eileen Paisley, later privately visits the McGuinness home to show solidarity with the family.

Alastair Campbell, Blair's spin doctor during the years when New Labour dominated British politics, described McGuinness as 'tough-minded, abrupt, likeable, human'. Campbell travelled to Derry to attend the funeral and speak with the McGuinness family.

Tony Blair, who played such a key role with McGuinness in helping to push the mainstream republican movement into constitutional politics, paid this telling tribute: 'Once he became the peacemaker, he became it wholeheartedly and with no shortage of determined opposition to those who wanted to carry on the war. I will remember him therefore with immense gratitude for the part he played in the peace process, and with genuine affection for the man I came to know and admire for his contribution to peace.'

© Derek Speirs

Shops and schools closed in Derry as thousands turned out to attend the funeral as it made its way from the McGuinness home to St Columba's church. The event is the closest Derry has ever come to a state funeral. Irish musicians lend their voices to the occasion, with Frances Black singing 'Raglan Road' outside St Columba's beside the coffin. Much later, at the graveside, Christy Moore sings 'The Time Has Come'.

Among those attending the funeral is Arlene Foster, first minister until the power-sharing executive collapsed at the start of 2017. Mourners applauded her as she entered the church, and Clinton referred to her presence at the Mass: 'I want to say a special word of appreciation to First Minister Foster for being here because I know and most people in this church know that your life has been marked in painful ways by the Troubles,' he said. 'And I believe the only way a lasting peace can ever take hold and endure is if those who have legitimate griefs on both sides embrace the future together.'

In another highly symbolic scene, as mourners filed out, Foster and Michelle O'Neill reached across the church pews to shake hands. It was a gesture that surely Martin McGuinness would have approved of.

Another of the main speakers at the requiem mass was Martin McGuinness's good friend the Presbyterian minister David Latimer. 'At some point in future I'm looking forward ... to praising God with him in heaven,' he said. Among the other Protestant clergymen to attend the funeral was the Methodist Harold Good. Good had been one of the two Irish religious leaders whom the IRA had agreed to have

© Dan Kitwood / Getty Images

as overseers of the decommissioning of the organisation's weapons. Reflecting on his friendship with McGuinness some time after the funeral, Good said he regarded himself and McGuinness as 'soul mates'. Movingly, he remembered bringing the already ill McGuinness up to his holiday home in Ballycastle, County Antrim, to a beauty spot with a view to Rathlin. Overwhelmed by the sight of the island out in the sea, McGuinness asked the Methodist minister, 'Is this where you go when you die?'

On the day of the funeral Father Michael Canny, who officiated at the service, told mourners that 'there are people in this church today whose presence would have been unthinkable only a generation ago ... They have forged working relationships with Martin McGuinness. They have built friendships with him. They have occupied Stormont's benches alongside him. Some have even sat in government with him. You are all very, very welcome.'

Prior to the funeral, Barack Obama issued a statement praising McGuinness as a 'man who had the wisdom and courage to pursue reconciliation for his people'. But it was Obama's Democrat predecessor Bill Clinton who took centre stage in delivering the main tribute to Martin McGuinness. Appealing for compromise between unionism and nationalism, Clinton told mourners: 'If you want to continue his legacy, go and finish the work he has started.' Clinton also joked that McGuinness was 'married' to Gerry Adams for nearly as long as he was to his wife Bernie, which provoked laughter both inside and outside St Columba's. Then referring to the McGuinness–Paisley friendship, Clinton noted that while he barely ever got through to the latter during political negotiations, 'it was great he [McGuinness] got a word in edgeways. I never could.' As the mourners filed out of the church, Clinton laid his hand on the tricolour-draped coffin to say goodbye.

A month after the funeral his family and party unveiled the headstone at his grave in Derry, where Mary Lou McDonald, the Sinn Féin deputy leader, gave another graveside oration. The inscription on his gravestone reads:

In proud and loving memory of Óglach Martin McGuinness
Óglaigh na h-Éireann
MP MLA Minister
Died 21st March 2017
Forever Loved, Bernie, Children & Grandchildren.

© AFP / Getty Images

'I will always be very proud to be from the Bogside. I have ended up
in many places throughout the world, the White House on countless
occasions, the Oval Office on three occasions with three American
presidents, and with prime ministers and presidents all over the place,
but my heart lies in the Bogside and with the people of Derry.'

Martin McGuinness, 1950–2017